Heavy, Heavier, Heaviest

amicus
readers

Ideas for Parents and Teachers

Amicus Readers let children practice reading informational texts at the earliest reading levels. Familiar words and concepts with close photo-text matches support early readers.

Before Reading
- Discuss the cover photo with the child. What does it tell him?
- Ask the child to predict what she will learn in the book.

Read the Book
- "Walk" through the book and look at the photos. Let the child ask questions.
- Read the book to the child, or have the child read independently.

After Reading
- Use the photo quiz at the end of the book to review the text.
- Prompt the child to make connections. Ask: *Can you think of other objects that are different weights?*

Amicus Readers are published by Amicus
P.O. Box 1329, Mankato, MN 56002
www.amicuspublishing.us

Library of Congress Cataloging-in-Publication Data
Felix, Rebecca, 1984-
  Heavy, heavier, heaviest / Rebecca Felix.
    pages cm. -- (Size it up)
  Audience: K to Grade 3.
  Audience: Age 6
  ISBN 978-1-60753-576-8 (hardcover) --
ISBN 978-1-60753-614-7 (pdf ebook)
 1. English language--Adjective--Juvenile literature. 2. English language--Comparison--Juvenile literature.
3. Vehicles--Juvenile literature. I. Title.
 PE1241.F4625 2014
   428.2--dc23
                          2013046272

Photo Credits: Photo Credits: BobJohns/Shutterstock Images, cover (top left), 1 (top left); Ccallanan/Shutterstock Images, cover (top right), 1 (top right); Yeko Photo Studio/Shutterstock Images, cover (bottom), 1 (bottom); iStockphoto, 3, 10, 11, 16 (top left); Sommai/Shutterstock Images, 4 (left); Ingram Publishing/Thinkstock, 4 (right); Blend Images/SuperStock, 5; Georgiy Pashin/Dreamstime, 6-7; Ryan McVay/Thinkstock, 8 (left), 16 (bottom left); Africa Studio/Shutterstock Images, 8-9, 16 (bottom middle); Michael C. Gray/Shutterstock Images, 9, 16 (bottom right); M. Unal Ozmen/Shutterstock Images, 12 (left); Peter Zijlstra/Shutterstock Images, 12 (right); Glenda/Shutterstock Images, 13; Kitch Bain/Shutterstock Images, 14 (left); Shutterstock Images, 14 (right); Alexander Raths/Shutterstock Images, 15; Le Do/Shutterstock Images, 16 (top middle); An Nguyen/Shutterstock Images, 16 (top right)

Produced for Amicus by The Peterson Publishing Company and Red Line Editorial.

Editor Jenna Gleisner
Designer Craig Hinton
Printed in the United States of America
Mankato, MN
2-2014
PA10001
10 9 8 7 6 5 4 3 2 1

Heavy objects have great weight. What heavy objects do you lift during the day?

A big glass of milk is heavy. A carton of milk is heavier. A gallon of milk is the heaviest. It takes two hands to lift it.

carton

glass

MILK

VITAMIN D
MILK

VITAMIN D
MILK

VITAMIN D
MILK

Great Tasting!

Great Tasting!

HALF GALLON (1.89 L)

HALF GALLON (1.89 L)

gallon

A 5-pound (2 kg) weight in gym class is heavy. An 8-pound (4 kg) weight is heavier. A 10-pound (5 kg) weight is the heaviest. It weighs more than a gallon of milk.

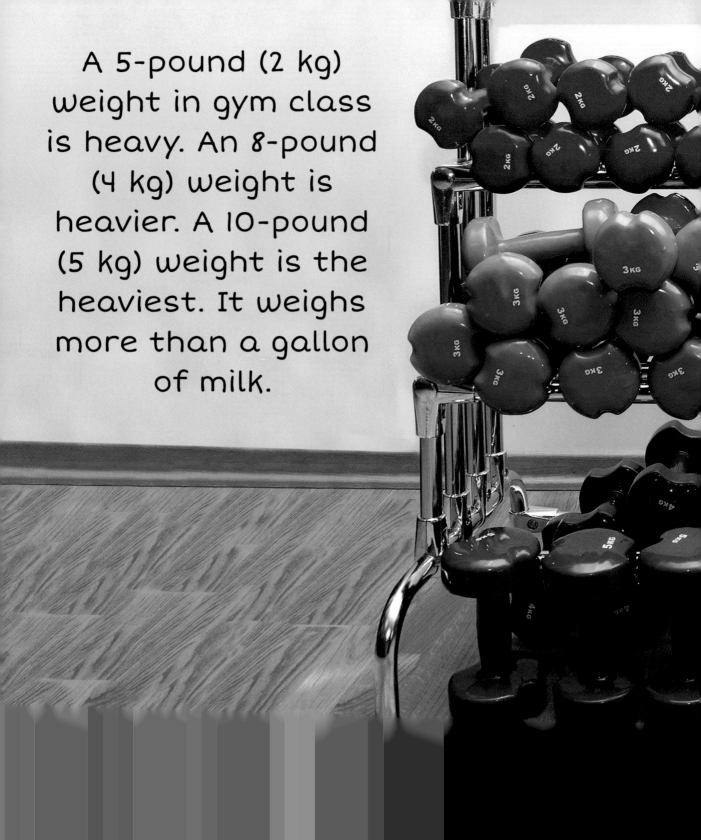

A textbook at school is heavy. A stack of books is heavier. A backpack full of books is the heaviest. It is too heavy to carry home.

textbook

stack of books

backpack

We lift heavy foods at the market. A cantaloupe is heavy. A watermelon is heavier. This giant pumpkin is the heaviest. It is almost too heavy for the scale!

watermelon

cantaloupe

pumpkin

A bag of flour is heavy. A bag of potatoes is heavier. This big bag of dog food is the heaviest. It weighs as much as eight bags of flour.

bag of potatoes

bag of flour

bag of
dog food

13

We lift heavy objects in the garden. A shovel is heavy. A hose is heavier. This wheelbarrow full of dirt is the heaviest. It is too heavy to lift by myself!

hose

shovel

wheelbarrow

Which object is the heaviest in each group?

pumpkin

cantaloupe

watermelon

textbook

stack of books

backpack